CONTE

SECTION 1 — HOW THIS ACTION PACK CAN HELP YOU
It's never too late to start planning for retirement. Take stock of your finances and review your living arrangements now *2*

SECTION 2 — TIMING
The financial pros and cons of taking early or late retirement. Benefits; NI contributions. How to go about claiming your state pension *3*

SECTION 3 — YOUR PENSION
A rundown on the three types of pension: state pensions, employers' (occupational) pension schemes and personal pension plans *6*

SECTION 4 — DOING THE SUMS
Comparing how much you spend now with how much you are likely to spend when you retire. Assessing your future income from pensions and other sources *11*

SECTION 5 — BOOSTING YOUR INCOME
Investing in your pension. A lump sum – should you take one? A range of tax-efficient investments. Alternative strategies. Ways of reducing your tax bill in retirement *15*

SECTION 6 — YOUR HOME
What are your priorities now, and might they change in due course? Staying put? Moving? *24*

SECTION 7 — LOOKING TO THE FUTURE
Long-term planning issues: inflation – how to fight back; your home – ways to make it safe, secure and convenient now; sheltered housing; making a will – how to keep inheritance tax to a minimum *29*

SECTION

II

HOW THIS ACTION PACK CAN HELP YOU

For most people, retirement is an exciting and fulfilling period of their lives. After a lifetime of work and maybe bringing up a family, at long last there is time to devote to yourself – your interests and friends, travelling, and so on.

But to take full advantage of the benefits that retirement from full-time employment can bring, planning is essential. Ten, or even 15, years before is not too soon to start. And you have to bear in mind that your retirement could last a long time – 20 or 30 years is not unusual these days, especially for those who take early retirement.

While such matters as health, mental attitude, and having interests, friends and family are extremely important, you can't always do much to influence them. However, the chances of a happy and fulfilling retirement will certainly be greater if you have planned your finances so that you're not having to worry constantly about every pound.

This Pack will help you to:

- think about your finances in the future by looking at what pension you're likely to get and what your spending might be after retirement
- decide how to bridge any gap between your income and your outgoings
- start thinking about where you want to live when you stop work
- look to the distant future when your income will have fallen behind your spending as a result of inflation and your housing needs may have altered.

It's never too late

While ideally you should start pension planning in your 30s or even your 20s, and should certainly have checked that in your 40s you were on course to provide for a comfortable retirement, it's hardly ever too late to improve the situation. Working through this Pack, in particular the section on *Boosting your income*, will give you a good start on your planning, even if you are already in your late 50s.

Remember inflation

Whenever you're looking at money for the future, bear in mind the effects of inflation. The table below shows how the buying power (in terms of today's money) of £1,000 shrinks as the years pass.

After:	inflation per year at:		
	4%	7%	10%
1 year	962	935	909
2 years	925	873	826
3 years	889	816	751
4 years	855	763	683
5 years	822	713	621
6 years	790	666	564
7 years	760	623	513
8 years	731	582	467
9 years	703	544	424
10 years	676	508	386

SECTION 2

TIMING

While you may simply assume you'll go on working until 'normal' retirement age, you might be considering early (or even late) retirement. What are the pros and cons? And how do you actually retire and get your pension?

EARLY RETIREMENT

No matter how early you retire, you cannot receive your **state pension** until you reach official state pension age – 65 for men, 60 for women.

Your occupational pension

Occupational pension schemes vary: some will allow you to retire early and take a smaller pension, others will not. Under Inland Revenue rules, pension schemes can allow employees to retire on maximum pension at any time from the age of 50 as long as they have been a member of the scheme for at least 20 years. (New rules mean that women can stay at work until they're 65 and get no less favourable pension terms than men with a similar work and contribution record.)

Inevitably, though, if you retire early you will get a smaller pension than if you had continued working until normal pension age. Not only will you have contributed less to the scheme, but your contributions will have had less time to build up so that a smaller fund is available to buy a pension. If your pension is based on your final salary it will almost certainly be smaller if you retire early.

But, to some extent, the effect early retirement has on your pension depends on the reason. If it is the result of ill health, your occupational pension may not be reduced, but that depends on the rules of the scheme. Equally, if you are offered early retirement because your employer is having to reduce the number of employees, the chances are that you will not lose out financially. However, if you choose to retire early for other reasons you are unlikely to do as well. Your pension could be reduced by a third if you retire five years early.

Your personal pension

You can choose to take your pension at any age from 50, though this depends on the terms of your particular plan. But you'll get less money than you would if you leave it until later to retire as your fund will have had less time to build up. But there's nothing to stop you having several plans from which you start to draw a pension at different times, perhaps starting in your late 50s and continuing until you are 70.

=**ACTION**= Before deciding to take early retirement:

- check whether you've paid enough contributions to get a full basic state pension when you retire (see p8)
- find out what occupational or personal pension you'll get (see p9)

- work through the steps in *Doing the sums* (p11) and, if necessary, *Boosting your income* (p15).

Other financial help

You may be able to claim **unemployment benefit** if you are prepared to sign that you are available for, and actively looking for, a job. If you took voluntary early retirement you will probably be disqualified from receiving benefit for 26 weeks. In addition, if you are 55 or over and get an occupational or personal pension, your benefit will be reduced by the amount by which your pension exceeds £35 a week. You claim by going along to the nearest unemployment benefit office; you will then have to 'sign on' every two weeks.

=*ACTION*= Get leaflet NI12 (see insert E in the back pocket of this Pack) or visit your local Citizens Advice Bureau.

If you are retiring early because of ill health you may be able to claim **invalidity benefit** (which is tax-free and can be paid until you're 70 for men and 65 for women). This is paid if you're still unable to work after 28 weeks of Statutory Sick Pay (SSP) from your employer or sickness benefit. If you don't get a transfer form from your employer or automatically start receiving invalidity benefit, contact your local Department of Social Security (DSS). At some point you will be examined by a DSS doctor. If you don't agree with a decision, for example that you are fit for work, you can appeal against it.

If you are disabled or chronically ill, you may be able to get other state benefits such as attendance or mobility allowance.

=*ACTION*= Get leaflets NI16A *Invalidity Benefit* and FB28 *Sick or Disabled?* from your local DSS, or visit your Citizens Advice Bureau.

Your NI contributions

Men automatically get NI contributions credited once they reach 60. And you'll get credits if you're claiming unemployment or invalidity benefit. Or Home Responsibility Protection might apply (see p6). All these keep up your contributions towards your basic pension.

If none of this applies, you should consider making voluntary contributions to maximise your basic pension when you do reach pension age. See p15 for advice on this.

LATE RETIREMENT

Check with your employer what happens if you go on working after normal pension age. Will you continue to pay contributions to the pension scheme and will you get a higher pension when you do eventually retire? With a personal pension plan your fund will simply go on growing and you may even be able to put off getting a pension until you're 75 if you like.

As far as your state pension is concerned, you can draw it and keep on working at the same time. Or you can defer claiming it, in which case the amount you get when you eventually retire is increased by 1% for every seven weeks that you work beyond retirement age, i.e. by 7.4% a year. By deferring your state pension by the maximum five years you'll increase it by just over one third. But you would be better off claiming it and investing it yourself.

If you are thinking of working after retirement, see the relevant section of *Boosting your income* on p15.

THE NUTS AND BOLTS

Having decided when you're going to retire, how do you actually go about it?

Claiming your state pension

You will automatically be sent a claim form (BR1) by the Department of Social Security about four months before normal pension age and you can make your claim immediately. If you delay claiming, your pension can be backdated for up to twelve months. You will then be sent a statement of your pension entitlement and how it is made up. If you are expecting a 'Guaranteed Minimum Pension' GMP (see p7) for periods for which you were contracted out of State Earnings Related Pension Scheme (SERPS – also see p7) the statement will tell you the name and address of the company (or companies) paying it. The statement will also tell you how to challenge any of the facts if you disagree with them. You have the right to take such questions to an independent tribunal if you can't reach agreement with the DSS.

You can choose how you want your pension to be paid. You can either:

- have it paid into your bank or building society account every four weeks or every quarter in arrears. See leaflet NI105 (details on insert E in the back pocket) *or*
- receive it weekly by cashing in orders at the post office of your choice. You don't have to collect your pension each week as the orders are valid for up to three months.

If you don't get your pension straight away, or if what you get seems low, check with the DSS. It is possible that they are still working out your entitlement and will pay any arrears as soon as their calculations are finished.

SECTION 3

YOUR PENSION

One of the key elements in the run-up to retirement is finding out how much pension you'll be getting. It's only when you've done this and looked at your likely spending that you'll be able to see whether there's a gap between your income and outgoings and can work out a strategy for plugging it.

You should get estimates from the various pension providers – see below. While these will be estimates of what you'll get at retirement age, they will be in terms of today's value of the pound. Don't worry about this. Later you'll be looking at your retirement spending and estimating this, too, in terms of today's pound, and as long as both estimates are on the same basis there's no problem.

YOUR STATE PENSIONS

Women can receive their state pension at 60, men at 65. Your state pension could include three elements – basic pension, graduated pension and SERPS pension.

Basic pension

You'll get this in full if you have paid or have been credited with National Insurance (NI) contributions for about 90% of your working life (which is defined as 49 years for a man, 44 years for a woman).

The NI contributions which count are:

- Class 1 – paid by employees. But reduced rate contributions paid by some married women don't count
- Class 2 – paid by self-employed people
- Class 3 – voluntary contributions (p15)
- Credits – for times when you've been claiming certain state benefits, such as when you're ill or looking after an invalid, unemployed or claiming maternity benefits. Men aged 60 or over who are not working, for instance because they have taken early retirement, get credits towards their basic pension
- Home Responsibility Protection – not strictly speaking a 'credit', but for every year for which you get child benefit for a child under 16 or are looking after someone who gets attendance allowance, your 'working life' (see above) is reduced by one year.

Details of basic state pension rates are given on insert F in the back pocket of this Pack. You'll get a reduced pension if your NI record is not good enough for a full pension – what you get will be in proportion to the number of years of NI that count. You could be in this position if you started work in your 20s after further education.

A married woman can get a state pension based on her own NI record, or that of her husband, whichever is the greater.

At present, the state pension is increased each year in line with inflation as shown by the Retail Prices Index (RPI).

Graduated pension

This was an earnings-related pension scheme which ran from April 1961 to April 1975. You would have paid graduated NI contributions in any week in which you earned more than £9 and it's these contributions which have built up your pension. Graduated pension won't make a vast difference to your income. For example, in 1989 the most you could have received was £255 a year for a man and £213 for a woman (the amount increases each year in line with inflation).

State Earnings Related Pension Scheme (SERPS)

This scheme for employees started in April 1978 and the pension you get is based on your earnings from then until retirement. The earnings which matter are those between a lower and an upper limit – in the 1989–90 tax year £43 and £325 a week. These limits are changed each year. Before calculating your pension, your earnings are revalued in line with the way average earnings have increased so that some allowance is made for inflation (though of earnings rather than prices).

The maximum SERPS pension anyone can receive in 1989–90 is about £35 a week – to get this you'd have to have earned at least at the rate of the upper earnings limit since 1978.

Your SERPS pension will be paid with your basic and graduated pensions, and the amount you get will increase in line with inflation.

Contracted out of SERPS?

Some employers decided that their own pension schemes were good enough for their employees not to have to contribute to SERPS. If you belong to one of these contracted-out pension schemes, you will have paid lower than normal NI contributions and will not get a SERPS pension for that time. Instead, if your employer runs a 'final pay' scheme (see p8), the minimum pension you get will be equivalent to SERPS (Guaranteed Minimum Pension). If your employer runs a contracted-out 'money purchase' scheme (p8), you will get certain basic pension rights (protected rights) instead of SERPS.

You might have chosen to contract out of SERPS since July 1988 by taking out a personal pension plan. If you did this, your NI contributions did not change, but after the end of each tax year, a proportion of what you had paid in contributions was paid into your pension plan. When you retire the amount of money invested for you will provide a pension which will be inflation-linked in the same way as SERPS.

Self-employed?

You will get the basic state pension if you have paid enough NI contributions. But you won't be entitled to any graduated pension or SERPS except for periods during which you were working as an employee and paying Class 1 NI contributions.

How to check your state pension

The Department of Social Security will give you a pension forecast of your basic, graduated and SERPS entitlement at pension age, based on the NI contributions you've paid so far and those you're likely to pay in the future. If you are (or have been) contracted out of SERPS, you will be told what SERPS you can expect after making deductions for your Guaranteed Minimum Pension (GMP) or other contracted-out pension.

=**ACTION**= Fill in form BR19 (there's a copy in the back pocket) and send it to the address at the top of the form. You'll get a forecast of your full state pension rights together with details of the deductions for contracted-out pensions.

Fill in form NP38 (there's also a copy in the back pocket) if you want further details of your SERPS entitlement.

EMPLOYERS' PENSION SCHEMES

Many employers run their own pension schemes to benefit their employees in retirement. Depending on the way the scheme works, you will get either a pension which is at least as big as the SERPS it replaces (if it's a contracted-out scheme) or a further pension on top of your state pensions. Whichever type of scheme it is, your pension will usually be paid for by your own contributions and those made by your employer, although some schemes are non-contributory, which means that only the employer makes contributions.

In order to qualify for the various tax exemptions, pension schemes have to conform to Inland Revenue rules, e.g.:

- the normal retirement age is between 60 and 75 (though schemes can allow for retirement on maximum pension at any time from the age of 50 for those who have been a member of the scheme for at least 20 years, or may set a minimum age, say, 62). Early retirement may be allowed in certain circumstances such as ill health
- the maximum pension cannot be more than two thirds of your final pay at normal retirement age
- although part of the pension can be swapped for a tax-free lump sum, this can't be more than one and a half times your final pay.

Final pay schemes

These are the most common type. How much pension you get depends on how many years you were in the scheme and on how much you earn in the last year or the last few years before your retirement. How earnings are defined can differ: some schemes will include bonuses, overtime and commission, but others will not. Typically, you'll get either one sixtieth or one eightieth of your 'final pay' for each year you've been in the scheme. So, if you have been a member of a scheme for 20 years, your pension will be twenty sixtieths (one third) or twenty eightieths (one quarter) of your final pay.

Money purchase schemes

These are the other common type. A money purchase scheme doesn't guarantee a pension related to your pay before retirement. Instead, the contributions made by you and your employer are invested. When you retire the money that has accumulated in your 'fund' is used to buy your pension. So the pension you get depends on what contributions have been paid, the length of time the money has had to 'grow', how well the investments do, and the interest rates at the time you retire.

▬ Other types of pension scheme

A **hybrid** scheme is basically a money purchase scheme but also guarantees that your pension at retirement will not be less than a certain proportion of your final pay.

With an **average earnings** scheme, your pension is worked out as a proportion of your average earnings over the whole time you contributed. In a **flat rate** scheme, everyone in the company receives the same pension (regardless of earnings), depending only on how many years they have worked there. These two are very uncommon these days.

▬ Deferred pensions

As well as the pension from your present employer, you may also be due a pension from one or more former employers (unless you took a refund of contributions or transferred the benefits to another pension scheme).

With a final pay scheme, your deferred pension will be based on what you were earning before you left the company. If this was some time ago, inflation is likely to have eaten away at its value. To counter this, any final pay pension you contributed to after January 1985 is automatically increased in line with inflation, though only to a maximum of 5% a year. If you left your job before that date, your pension will normally be frozen. Some schemes increase deferred pensions by more than the legal minimum.

With a money purchase scheme your money is simply left invested, and how well you do out of it depends on the factors explained earlier.

▬ Checking your occupational pension

If you haven't had a recent statement of the pension you can expect at retirement, ask the pensions manager for one. You will also find information in your pensions handbook or leaflet. The sort of questions you want answers to might include those in the box on the next page.

=**ACTION**= Ask for a statement from your current pension scheme (and schemes to which you've contributed in the past) if you haven't received one recently.

=**ACTION**= Check you have all the details about your pension that you need to plan your future finances. To help with this, work through the list overleaf. If there are points neither your statement nor your pensions handbook mention, ask the pension scheme administrators.

▬ PERSONAL PENSION PLANS

If you're self-employed or employed but not a member of the firm's pension scheme, you may have been paying into a pension plan run by an institution such as an insurance company or bank in order to provide income in your retirement. If you started contributing before July 1988, the scheme would have operated under the old rules. Such schemes are often referred to as *section 226* pension plans.

New-style personal pension plans have been available since July 1988 and all employees have been able to choose a personal pension rather than paying into their employer's scheme.

3

9

All personal pension plans work on the money purchase principle: your contributions are invested and the accumulated fund is used to buy you an annuity from an insurance company or friendly society, which provides you with an income for life. The amount of pension you get depends on how well your contributions have been invested and on interest rates at the time you get your pension.

You have rather more choice with personal pensions than with occupational pensions. You can retire when you like (within limits): with an old-style plan you can get your pension from 60; with a new plan you can get your pension at 50. However, the younger you are when you get your pension, the smaller your pension will be. You can also be more flexible about the amount you take as a lump sum (see p17).

Checklist of pension information

1. What pension will I get, assuming I work until normal pension age?
2. Can I retire any earlier than this, and if so what pension will I get?
3. Can I retire later than normal? If so, will I have to carry on paying contributions and will my pension be correspondingly increased when I do retire?
4. How will my pension increase after I have retired? Are the increases guaranteed or discretionary?
5. Can I take a lump sum when I retire? If so, what is the maximum, and what effect will this have on my pension?
6. Is my pension scheme contracted out of SERPS?
7. How much pension will my widow/er get? Will this increase?
8. If a widow/er's pension isn't provided, can one be arranged? If so, what effect will it have on my pension?
9. How will my pension be paid: into my bank or by post? When will I get it: on the first of each month? How often: monthly or quarterly?
10. If I make extra contributions, what benefit will I get for them, and will they increase my pension, provide a pension for my widow/er, or what?

SECTION 4

DOING THE SUMS

To find out how you are going to manage financially once you have retired, you should start by examining your spending now. Once you've done this, work out how it might change when you've stopped working. You can then compare the estimates of your spending and income after retirement – and look at ways of plugging the gap (if there is one).

TODAY'S SPENDING

Your aim is to work out where your money is likely to go in the next 12 months. The more accurate you can be, the more useful the results.

The first stage is to assemble the information. For major and regular items of expenditure (mortgage payments, gas bills, insurance premiums etc), look at what you've spent in the last 12 months and adjust the figures to take into account expected or known changes. You'll probably find the details you need in your bank or building society statements, cheque book stubs, credit card statements, bills paid, receipts and so on.

But a lot of your day-to-day spending won't be accounted for in this way. You'll know that you have written cheques to certain firms, used your credit card for other purchases and made cash withdrawals, but you are unlikely to remember precisely what you bought. Rather than guessing (which is likely to underestimate the real figures), we recommend that you keep a record of what you spend for a month or so. Carry a notebook with you all the time and write down how much you spend and what you spend it on. You can then project your spending for the rest of the year, making necessary adjustments for holidays and special expenses such as Christmas and seasonal variations.

ACTION Fill in the columns headed 'Your spending now' in the *Spending Calculator* (worksheet A in the back pocket of this Action Pack).

To do this you'll need to sort out your spending under a number of different headings – as many as will be useful to you. We've divided spending into categories in a particular way but there is no need for you to follow this plan exactly. But however you decide to analyse your spending, there are some points to bear in mind.

Monthly or yearly spending?

It's useful to put figures in both columns, although you might find it easier to visualise a lot of your spending in monthly terms. If you think in terms of weekly spending, remember that there are 52 weeks in a year!

Household equipment

What you spend on replacing and repairing domestic equipment such as your washing machine, dishwasher, TV or stereo will vary considerably from year to year. But try to look at what you've spent over the last five years, get an idea of current costs and make a stab at working out an average figure.

▬ *Your car*

If you own a car the costs of running and owning it may appear considerable (and appear on your bills). But what doesn't appear is the amount by which it depreciates in value. While this isn't 'spending' in the sense that money is going out of your bank account each month, ideally you should be saving a sum each year to provide the extra you're going to need when you buy your next car.

▬ *One-off spending*

This can be predictable (such as a new bathroom) or out of the blue (such as having to replace a roof which your insurance company won't pay for). All you can do here is to estimate a typical figure for one-off spending, averaged over the years.

▬ TOMORROW'S SPENDING

Once you have retired, there will be changes to your spending pattern even if you don't intend to make any major changes in your lifestyle.

For example, you might spend less (or nothing) on:

- -£ your mortgage (as you're likely to have paid it off)
- -£ pension and/or NI contributions
- -£ travelling to work e.g. train or bus fares, or petrol, parking etc
- -£ formal clothes for work
- -£ lunches, drinks and general socialising at work

- -£ having work done for you at home such as housework, d-i-y, gardening, decorating
- -£ school or university fees (assuming your children have finished their education by the time you retire).

On the other hand, you might spend more on:

- +£ heating your home (because you spend more time there)
- +£ entertainment (inviting friends in, going to the theatre, concerts etc more often)
- +£ holidays (as you are no longer limited to, say, three weeks)
- +£ hobbies and other interests
- +£ food (if you've had subsidised or free meals, coffee, tea etc at work)
- +£ your car (if you've been used to having a company car but now want your own).

=**ACTION**= Fill in the columns headed 'Your spending after retirement' in the *Spending Calculator* (worksheet A) using the figures for your current spending as a reference. Think about reasons why your spending might change – there's space to write down a brief description of them. Then fill in the figures with your projected post-retirement spending figures. Obviously you can give only estimates, but with careful thought these should at least be realistic.

There are some points you should bear in mind:

▬ *Living it up*

As you won't yet be able to assess how much time or money you'll be spending on such items as holidays and hobbies the simplest solution is to decide what you would like ideally to be able to spend and use this as your starting point.

12

▬ *Your car*

This is one area of spending that could be very different when you retire. Of course, you could decide not to have a car and use public transport and taxis (though you should check what is available first).

But many people will want to run a car. If you have been used to having a company car you will be faced with the considerable costs of owning and running your own. Try to make realistic estimates of the costs – perhaps using *Which?* reports on cars as a guide. Even if you haven't had a company car there may be changes in the mileage you do (it could go up or down), which will mean more or less spending on petrol, repairs and servicing.

▬ TOMORROW'S INCOME

Having tried to estimate what you're likely to spend when you have retired, you then need to estimate what income you're going to get.

▬ *Pensions*

If you've worked through the *Pensions* section of this Action Pack you will already know how to check how much you'll get from the various types of pension you're expecting.

=ACTION= Fill in the pensions details of the *Your Income after Retirement* (worksheet B) in the pocket at the back of this Action Pack. Use gross amounts (i.e. the pensions income before tax is deducted).

▬ *Other income*

You need to make an estimate of your income from sources other than your pensions. You should work in terms of today's value of the pound as this is the basis on which your pensions will be estimated. One problem with estimating income from investments over the long term is that some investment income may at least keep pace with inflation, e.g. share and unit trust dividends, whereas other income, such as that from building society savings, will not.

As we've designed this Action Pack for people who are relatively close to retirement, inflation shouldn't be too big a problem, so we suggest that you should think in terms of the income you're getting at the moment from investments, making only adjustments that you expect. For example, if you know you will get a lump sum from a life insurance policy before you retire and intend to invest this, you can include this income.

We've listed other sources of income in various groups:

Income not taxed before you get it This could include interest from National Savings accounts, income and capital bonds and interest on British Government Stock bought on the National Savings Stock Register.

UK share dividends and unit trust distributions Also include interest on British Government stocks that is paid after deduction of basic rate tax. Add the amount of tax that has already been deducted – this will be shown on tax vouchers you get from whoever pays you the income.

Any other taxable income This is where you put such things as earnings from a job, consultancy, freelance work, own business, rents from property, etc (having deducted allowable expenses first).

Interest from UK banks (including finance companies), building societies and local authority loans The interest is paid to you after deduction of basic rate tax so you have to 'gross up' the interest by dividing what you get by 0.75.

=**ACTION**= Fill in the rest of the income section on worksheet B and add up the figures to give you your total taxable income.

One calculator or two?

If you're married, both partners should fill in a form. From April 1990 you will be treated as two separate people by the taxman. Each of you will have your own personal allowance and a wife's investment income will be taxed as belonging to her (rather than to her husband).

▬ Your outgoings

Tax relief is available on certain spending, so when working out your income, outgoings have to be taken into account as they reduce your overall tax bill.

Mortgage interest paid net of tax under the MIRAS scheme You get tax relief on the interest paid on up to £30,000 worth of mortgage and will get this automatically if you pay under MIRAS. You need to enter the gross amount of interest paid, so ask the lender for this figure.

Other outgoings The list here should be self-explanatory, but again remember that it's the gross amount you should put down, not the net amount you pay.

=**ACTION**= Fill in the Outgoings section of worksheet B.

▬ Income tax

This form gives only a basic guide to income tax; for full details you may find the latest issue of the *Which? Tax-Saving Guide* helpful – see insert E in the back pocket for details.

Much of this part of the calculator is self-explanatory, though you'll have to do some sums to get details of your tax allowance.

=**ACTION**= Work through the *Allowance calculator* (insert C in the back pocket of this Action Pack) to enable you to fill in this part of worksheet B.

▬ The answer

The final bit of the calculation is simple. First, add up details of any **tax-free** income you receive. This could be from cashing in National Savings Certificates, up to £70 of interest from a National Savings Bank Ordinary Account or income from share dividends or unit trust distributions in a qualifying Personal Equity Plan. Add this amount to your total taxable income worked out in the first part.

Finally, deduct your income tax. What you're left with is your best estimate of your income after retirement.

=**ACTION**= Compare your income after retirement with your spending after retirement. If they match, or your income is higher than your spending – congratulations! If not, don't panic, but move on to *Boosting your income*.

14

SECTION 5

BOOSTING YOUR INCOME

When you've estimated what your income and spending will be when you retire you'll probably find there's a gap. Commonsense dictates two solutions to this problem – increasing your income and reducing your spending. As you have a few years to go to retirement it's sensible to start by seeing how you can plan to boost your income.

USING A PENSION SCHEME

Saving through a pension scheme – whether it's your employer's or some sort of personal pension plan – should be your first choice for extra savings because of the preferential tax treatment given to such schemes.

For a start, you get tax relief on your contributions. What this means is that if you pay tax at 25%, investing £100 in a pension scheme costs you only £75, with the taxman contributing the other £25. If you pay tax at 40% it costs you only £60, and the taxman chips in the other £40. Moreover, the pension schemes themselves pay no income tax or capital gains tax so your contributions build up faster than with most other forms of investment.

Because of these tax advantages, there are restrictions on how much you can invest:

- **employers' schemes** Your contributions (including AVCs – see below) are limited to 15% of your earnings from that job (including the taxable value of fringe benefits). In addition, your scheme can't provide a pension greater than two thirds of your income at retirement
- **personal pension scheme** Your maximum contributions depend on your age:

age on 6 April	maximum contributions in tax year as percentage of earnings
35 or less	17.5%
36–45	20%
46–50	25%
5–55	30%
56 or over	35%

(NB: Different rules apply for contributions made before the 1989–90 tax year)

Generally, if you pay into your employer's scheme, you can't pay into a personal plan as well (though you can have a 'minimum plan' solely for contracting out of SERPS (see p7). However, if you also have freelance earnings or run a small business you can have a personal pension plan and get tax relief on those contributions up to the limits shown above.

Investing more in pensions

All employers' pension schemes allow you to pay **Additional Voluntary Contributions (AVCs)** to top up your pension. For example, if you already pay 5% of your salary into your employer's pension scheme, you can put in another 10% as AVCs.

15

AVCs will be used to increase your pension but you can't swap any of the pension they build up for a lump sum unless you started paying AVCs before 6 April 1987. You may also be able to use AVCs to build up a pension for a dependant, but you'd have to check the rules of the pension scheme first.

Instead of paying AVCs into your employer's scheme you can pay them into a scheme you select, such as those run by insurance companies, banks, building societies and so on. These are called **freestanding AVCs (FSAVCs)**. Most schemes use your contributions to build up a fund which can then buy extra benefits when you retire. (Again, you can't use FSAVCs to increase the lump sum you get on retirement unless you started paying into the scheme before 6 April 1987.)

You can't use AVCs or FSAVCs to boost your pension at retirement above two thirds of your earnings at that time. But you can use them to add other benefits such as extra pension, extra widow's pension or extra increases to your pension once it's being paid. If your contributions (whether your basic contributions from salary, AVCs or FSAVCs) exceed the limits, you'll get the excess back (after a tax deduction broadly in line with the tax benefits given on it).

Employer's scheme or free-standing?

If you pay AVCs into your employer's scheme it's likely that more of your contributions will actually be invested on your behalf than if you choose a free-standing scheme. This is because the cost of running a FSAVC will effectively have to be paid from your contributions, whereas in your employer's scheme the costs will be paid by the employer. You might also find that your employer's scheme will provide a wider range of benefits for AVCs than FSAVCs.

But FSAVCs allow you to invest your money in different ways – for example, through a with-profits or unit-linked plan. With your employer's scheme you have no such choice.

=ACTION= Check how much of your salary is going in pension contributions and what benefits are being built up (see p10). Decide how much extra you can afford in contributions and arrange to pay these.

Increasing your personal pension

Simple – just put larger amounts into your pension. You can exceed the limits on contributions shown above and save a much larger percentage of your income if you have unused tax relief from any of the previous six years. But if you aren't counted as having unused relief for any period in which you were a member of an employer's scheme.

Finding a plan that suits you shouldn't be difficult whether you want to save each month, each year or make a series of one-off payments. The *Which?* Action Pack *Choose Your Pension* should help you with your decision (see insert E in the back pocket).

=ACTION= Check what pension contributions you've made over the last six tax years to see whether you can pay extra into a personal pension and still get tax relief.

16

Pension or lump sum?

Most pension schemes (employers' and personal) allow you to swap part of your pension for a tax-free lump sum. With some schemes, particularly in the public sector, you get a lump sum which you may be able to exchange for a pension.

The maximum lump sum you can take is:

- **employers' scheme** One and a half times your final earnings. There may also be a cash limit. If the scheme was set up before 17 March 1987 and hasn't been changed since that date there is no limit; if it was set up or altered between that date and 14 March 1989 there's a limit of £150,000, and if the scheme was set up after this date or you joined it after 1 June 1989, the maximum is £90,000 (though this will, however, be increased each year)
- **personal pension plan** If you have a plan set up before 1 July 1988 (a *section 226* policy) the biggest lump sum you can have is three times the maximum remaining pension the company could pay you. With a new-style pension plan (bought after 1 July 1988) the maximum is one quarter of your fund after certain amounts have been deducted. For example, if you used the personal pension plan to contract out of SERPS, the amount needed to buy your retirement pension in place of SERPS will be deducted.

If you're due to get a pension which is linked to inflation you should be wary of swapping any of it for a lump sum. Even if the increases aren't as good as this but are regular and substantial you should think carefully before going for a lump sum.

When deciding whether to take the lump sum, bear in mind the effect it will have on your pension and what you're going to do with it. As a guide, a man's pension is reduced by £100 a year for each £900 taken as a lump sum, and a woman's by £100 for each £1100. But if you use the cash to buy an annuity you could get a higher income than if you had left the money in your pension scheme. This is thanks to the favourable tax treatment of income from annuities (see p29). A better strategy might be to invest the money in something else when you retire and use that money to buy an annuity when you're older – you'll get a much better return and might need a boost to your income if it hasn't kept up with inflation.

Boosting your state pension

If your NI contribution record in any year is not good enough to count towards your basic pension, you can pay Class 3 (voluntary) contributions to make that year's record full. If you have paid some NI or been awarded credits for a tax year but not enough, the DSS will inform you by sending a statement some time after the end of the tax year. This will show the amount of Class 3 contributions needed to make the year count for your pension. You'll get a leaflet explaining how you should pay. You have up to six years to pay those contributions.

If you have received a pension forecast (having sent off form BR19 – there's a copy in the back pocket of the Pack) this will also tell you whether it's worth paying extra contributions.

If you're in any doubt, check with the DSS whether paying extra will increase your pension.

OTHER INVESTMENTS

Saving via a pension scheme should be your first choice for increasing your after-retirement income. But you may already be investing as much as you can in a pension scheme or may want to have more control and flexibility over some of your money than you get in a pension scheme.

Before doing anything, decide what you want from your money. If you want to increase your after-retirement income, think about investing to build up a capital sum. When you retire you can use this to provide an income – perhaps by buying an annuity (see p29).

What you choose will depend, to some extent, on how far you are from retirement. If you're within five years or so you may not be prepared to risk seeing the value of your investments fluctuate too much. If so, first consider investments where you'll always be able to get back what you put in – although the spending power of your capital may have been eroded by inflation.

Index-linked National Savings Certificates are one way of ensuring that your capital is protected from inflation. You can use them for lump sum or regular/intermittent savings; each certificate costs £25 but the maximum you can invest is £5,000. You'll get the best return by investing for five years, though can get your money back before. The proceeds are totally free of tax.

National Savings Certificates are similar, but there's no index-linking. Instead, you know at the outset exactly what your investment will be worth at the end of the five years. Again, the proceeds are tax-free.

Banks, finance companies and building societies offer a huge variety of accounts from interest-bearing current accounts to accounts where your money is tied up for a year or more. Interest rates vary considerably depending not only on how much you have to invest and how much notice you're prepared to give but also on which institution you invest with.

Guaranteed growth bonds sold by insurance companies do just what they say, i.e. your money grows at a fixed rate guaranteed for the life of the bond, which can be from one to ten years. But you can't normally get at your money before the end of the fixed period.

If you're planning to retire in five to ten years (or don't want to use your invested money until then) you should be thinking about a wider range of investments. Then some of your money will be tucked away safely, while another portion is in investments which, over the longer term, have a better chance of beating inflation. But going for higher returns means accepting that the value of your investment can fluctuate – downwards as well as up!

Shares If you want to spread your money into a variety of investments with varying degrees of risk, consider some form of investment in shares – either directly or via unit trusts or investment trusts.

The costs of buying and selling and the need to have a spread of shares mean you shouldn't think of buying shares directly unless you plan to invest £7,500 to £10,000. Unit trusts are suitable for smaller sums and many have plans for regular savings, so will be a better choice for smaller sums. You could also consider investment trusts.

Personal Equity Plans (PEPs) are a tax-efficient way of investing in shares or unit trusts. The income from PEPs is free of income tax, and no capital gains tax is due on any proceeds when you sell. You can't invest more than £4,800 a year in PEPs.

Before deciding to invest in any form of scheme make sure you know (and understand) all the terms and conditions attached to the investment:

- what rate of return will you get (dividends or interest)?
- will the interest be paid out as income or left to increase the value of your capital?
- is your money tied up for a set period?
- will you have to pay a penalty if you take your money out early?
- what costs and charges (if any) will you have to pay?

Getting advice

If you want help in investing your money, you'll find may people willing to help, e.g. independent investment advisers, your bank or building society, your accountant or solicitor, stockbrokers, brokers and so on. All businesses giving advice on investments must be authorised under the Financial Services Act. While authorisation shows that a firm has proper financial backing, trained staff and is properly run, it doesn't mean that its advice will necessarily be good (though you do have some comeback and the possibility of compensation if things go wrong).

To have the best chance of getting good advice you need to have done your homework first so that you know what it is you want from your money, and get opinions from several advisers to compare what they say. *Which? Way to Save and Invest* will help you do this (see insert E for details).

ALTERNATIVE STRATEGIES

What if you don't have spare money to save for your retirement? Don't despair. There are alternatives – and you could set these up now, before you retire.

Working

You might consider working after retiring from your main job. As well as increasing your income, it can help to bridge the gap between full-time work and full-time leisure which can be a difficult period for you and your family.

You could stay in your present job (if your employer agrees) and defer taking your pension (see p9). But if you do want to earn some money, now could be the time to think about doing something completely different. Ask yourself some questions:

- why do you want to work – is it the money or the company of other people or the fear of having too little to do?
- how much time do you want to spend working – full-time, part-time regularly each week, or do you just want to be able to work at odd times that suit you?
- where do you want to work – locally, further afield or at home?
- do you want work in the same field as now, using your experience, training and contacts? Or do you want to strike out in a new direction, perhaps enlarging a hobby into a small business or using new skills?

Discuss these questions with your family – their reactions and own ideas will help you decide what you want. From then on it's a question of planning, learning and making contacts.

Be realistic about the contribution your work will make to your finances. Take advice – from a local enterprise agency if you want to set up a small business; from your professional body if you intend to stay in the same line of work; from Job Centres if you're going to be looking for a job; consult reference books at libraries; talk to contacts if you intend to act as a consultant or do freelance work. Doing this before retirement will mean you have laid the foundations for your new career.

One cautionary note: once you reach state pension age (60 for women, 65 for men) you no longer have to pay National Insurance Contributions. But any money you earn and any profits you make will be taxable.

Voluntary work

Whether you do some paid work after retirement or not, you could consider voluntary work. It can provide company, mental stimulation, a sense of involvement with the community and perhaps make all the difference to achieving a satisfying life after work.

Voluntary organisations provide opportunities for all sorts of involvement and are always looking for people to help. For example, you could advise in a Citizens Advice Bureau or other advice-giving agency, visit people in their own homes to provide company or to do practical jobs such as gardening or shopping, or bring your expertise to the running of an organisation by serving on a management committee.

Or you may have a local co-ordinating body for volunteers, such as a Volunteer Bureau which would have ideas on where you could offer help. (See also insert E in the back pocket.)

Pensions and retirement

Until October 1989 your basic state retirement pension would have been reduced if you had earned more than £75 per week or if you had worked full-time, but now you can earn and work as much as you like and still draw your pension in full. Likewise, earning money will have no effect on your occupational or personal pensions.

Letting your home

If your home is large enough, you could think about letting a room or two. Not only will you get extra income, but possibly also company and maybe some help around the house. On the other hand, if things don't turn out well, you could be involved in a legal battle to extract rent or to get your lodgers or tenants out. So it's not something to enter into without careful preparation and thought, or without well-drawn-up legal agreements.

There are three possible ways of letting your home: you could take in paying guests or lodgers to whom you provide at least one meal a day; you could let part of your home as self-contained accommodation to tenants, or you could rent your whole house while you live somewhere else.

Before letting any part of your home on any basis find out your legal rights (and those of your prospective lodgers or tenants). In particular, make sure you are clear on the procedure for getting rid of troublesome tenants. Ask your solicitor or contact your local Citizens Advice Bureau or Housing Advice Centre. If you draw up an agreement yourself, have it checked by a solicitor.

Also check up on the tax implications. You'll have to pay income tax on money you get from letting part or all of your home. But you can deduct many expenses such as repairs and decoration, the cost of services you provide, insurance and so on. Capital gains tax (CGT) could also be due when you sell your home, but not if you've just had lodgers who share your living space. If you've let your whole home or part of it, you could owe CGT depending on the proportion of the home that you have let and what length of time. Your solicitor or accountant should be able to advise, or consult the *Which? Tax-Saving Guide* (see insert E in the back pocket).

Finally, before taking strangers into your home, take up references from their bank (or building society) and from their employer (or college if they are students).

Holiday lets

If you have a holiday home or can convert outbuildings or part of your home as self-contained accommodation you could think about letting it out to people for their holidays. As long as the accommodation is available for letting on at least 140 days each year and actually let for 70 of those days you can treat the earnings in the same way as earnings from a business. This means you can set all the running expenses against the income you receive. If you're over 60 when you sell the property, the retirement relief rules may mean you will pay less CGT than you otherwise would.

TAX MATTERS

Your income after retirement will be taxed in much the same way as it was before. You will have to pay income tax on your pensions and on unearned income (such as interest received on investments), and you could have to pay capital gains tax when you dispose of things you own. There are, however, ways of reducing your tax bill.

Income tax

From the tax year in which you reach 65 (for both men and women) you get a higher personal allowance (a sum on which you pay no tax) than younger people. (Until the 1990–91 tax year, this was called 'Age allowance'.) If you're married you also get a higher married couple's allowance. However, if your total income (say, from an occupational pension and from investments) exceeds a certain limit, you begin to lose the extra tax-free allowance and eventually you receive just the ordinary personal allowance. For full details of how to check your allowances, see insert C in the back pocket of this Pack.

If your income is in the region where you start to lose some of your allowance you are effectively being taxed at a fairly high rate, 37.5%, on part of your income, so it makes sense to try to reduce your 'total income'. This is not what you think of as your income, but your taxable income after deducting certain outgoings. Tax-free income doesn't count towards this limit, so to maximise your tax allowance think about investing some of your savings in tax-free as opposed to taxable investments (though there isn't a lot of choice):

- National Savings certificates
- PEPs
- Friendly society savings.

Having an annuity can also be a way of saving your age allowance as only part of the annuity income is taxable – see p29.

Outgoings include mortgage interest and enforceable maintenance payments on which you can get tax relief, but you can't

21

really arrange to have these just to increase your allowance. However, if you give money to charities (either regularly or on an ad hoc basis), you could formalise this by making payments under covenant (or payroll-giving if you still work). That way you pay the charity the after-tax relief amount (say £75 if you've agreed to give £100: the charity collects the other £25 and your 'total income' for the purposes of your allowance is reduced by £100).

ACTION Work through the Allowance Calculator C and if you are losing out because your 'total income' is just over the limit, consider switching some of your investments and making covenants to reduce it.

Your state retirement pensions are taxable but tax isn't deducted before you get paid. But if you receive an occupational pension this is likely to be taxed under the PAYE system. In order to simplify tax gathering, the tax due on your state pension will also be deducted from your occupational pension. This will make it look as if you are paying tax at a very high rate. To be sure it's right, check your notice of coding. If you have any queries, contact your tax office.

Any earnings will also be taxable and again, if you work for an employer and earn more than a certain amount, you will pay tax under PAYE. If you are already getting all your tax-free allowances set against your pensions, you will pay tax on every pound you earn.

You have to pay income tax on your investments, unless they are tax-free, e.g. proceeds from SAYE or National Savings certificates, premium bond prizes and dividends or distributions from PEPs. If you have accounts with banks or building societies, the equivalent of basic rate tax is deducted from the interest before you receive it. You can't reclaim this even if your income isn't high enough for you to pay tax, but if you pay tax at the higher rate you will owe more tax. Other investments such as shares and unit trusts deduct basic rate tax before paying out dividends etc, but you can reclaim this if you're a non-taxpayer. Finally, a few investments pay interest without deducting any tax, and you will owe tax on these, e.g. National Savings income bonds.

ACTION From the 1990–91 tax year, husbands and wives will be taxed separately. If you're married, you should reorganise your investments to make sure the wife is able to make full use of her personal allowance.

Capital gains tax

If you sell goods or property (or dispose of them in another way, such as giving them away) and they're worth more than when you acquired them you might have to pay CGT. An indexation allowance takes inflation into account by linking the value of your assets to changes in the retail prices index (RPI). The first £5,000 of taxable capital gain in a tax year is tax-free but anything above that will be treated as if it was income – so you'll pay tax at basic or higher rate depending on what other income you have. From the 1990–91 tax year a husband and wife will each be able to make £5,000 of taxable gains a year before paying any CGT.

Gains on many items are never taxable, no matter how much you make:

- your only or main home
- private cars
- any item passed from husband to wife (or vice versa)
- proceeds from National Savings certificates, Yearly Plan, Capital Bonds
- premium bond prizes
- winnings from bets and pools

- proceeds from qualifying life insurance policies
- British Government stocks
- most personal belongings
- PEPs.

This isn't a full list of exemptions – the *Which? Tax-Saving Guide* gives further information (see insert E).

In addition, there are numerous special cases and reliefs. Of particular interest is retirement relief, which can reduce the tax payable when you dispose of part or all of your business if you are at least 60 and have owned the business for at least a year. The maximum retirement relief applies if you've owned your business for at least ten years, in which case you won't have to pay any CGT on the first £125,000 of gains and have to pay only half the CGT on gains between £125,000 and £500,000.

=**ACTION**= Try to keep your annual taxable gains to £5,000 (or less) to avoid CGT. Be sure to deduct all your allowable expenses such as improving the asset, the cost of advertising it or the cost of legal fees. If your losses come to more than your gains, you can carry them forward to next year. Unfortunately, you can't carry forward any gains!

SECTION 6

YOUR HOME

Is your dream to move to a thatched cottage with roses round the door when you finally put away your briefcase? Or do the beaches and siestas of sunny Spain seem desirable? Now's the time to be thinking seriously about where you plan to live after you've retired.

Ask yourself a few basic questions about your lifestyle and priorities for when you retire, such as:

- do you want to be close to your family and friends?
- will your present home be the right size when you retire? Will it give you enough space to do what you want to?
- do you want a bigger house – perhaps so you can see more of your family or take in guests?
- do you want a smaller house that needs less upkeep and cleaning?
- do you want a smaller/larger garden?
- do you want to move away from (or into) a busy urban area?
- what's wrong with your present home – can problems be put right or will they appear even more serious when you spend more time there? For instance, will the daytime noise from traffic, nearby school or factory be tolerable?
- do you want to release some of the money tied up in your house to give you more money to spend or to invest to provide an income?

These are only some of the questions, but it's worth spending some time thinking about your home and not feeling pressured into making a hasty decision when you do retire.

=ACTION= Draw up a list of what you want to do when you retire and the pros and cons of staying in your present home rather than moving.

STAYING PUT

If your home isn't quite what you want you could think about altering it as an alternative to moving. For example, you could re-organise your rooms, perhaps turning a spare bedroom into a room for activities such as d-i-y, painting or sewing. Or you could think about converting the loft or garage to provide an extra room. You might even consider having an extension built if your home doesn't provide the facilities you want.

As the chances are high that you'll spend more time at home once you've retired, think about ways in which you could make your home more comfortable (or cheaper to run). To minimise your heating bills check that your heating system is working efficiently – a new, modern boiler could save money in relatively few years. Check the insulation in the roof space and around the hot water cylinder; if it is in poor condition (or non-existent) update it. If you have no shower or ground-floor lavatory it might be sensible to install one. See p31 for things you could consider now to make your life easier when you're much older.

=ACTION= Get any major construction work or repairs done as soon as possible. You're likely to be better off financially in the years before retirement than after.

Your mortgage

If you have a mortgage it may have been planned to ensure that you finish paying it before you reach normal retirement age. But as more people retire early and lenders adopt a more flexible attitude, this pattern is starting to break down and an increasing number of people may still be paying their mortgage after they have retired.

How your mortgage loan will be paid off depends on its type:

- **repayment mortgage** You'll have been paying the loan off bit by bit over the whole length of the mortgage; with the last instalment the loan is repaid
- **endowment mortgage** The proceeds of the endowment policy should be enough to pay back the original loan (and may leave you with a lump sum)
- **pension mortgage** The lump sum you can take from your personal pension (see p17) repays the mortgage loan; the remainder of your pension fund buys your pension.

Should you repay early?

If you are due to receive your pension before your mortgage is paid, you may wonder whether to repay the loan using your lump sum. In general it may be worth doing this if you are paying a higher rate of interest on the loan than you would get if you invested the lump sum. Remember that you get tax relief (at your highest rate of income tax) on the interest on the first £30,000 of your loan. If the quoted mortgage rate is 15% and you pay tax at 25%, your mortgage is costing you only 11.25%, or only 9% if you pay tax at the higher rate.

If interest rates are favourable, you could think about paying back just part of the mortgage loan rather than the whole lot. Reducing the outstanding amount to £30,000 will maximise the effect of tax relief. And it may not be easy to invest your lump sum where it'll earn a high enough return to pay the interest on that part of the loan which is not subject to tax relief.

One complication is that the actual interest rate you pay on most repayment mortgages rises quickly in the last two or three years. For example, with a quoted mortgage rate of 15%, the effective after-tax relief interest rate in the early years is about 12%. This climbs steadily (but slowly) over the years until with three years left you are paying around 14% (remember, this is the cost *after* tax relief). In the last year or so the cost is a staggering 22.5%. If you ask your lenders they should be able to tell you the effective rate on your loan and take this into account in your decision.

Don't just pay off the loan because it sounds like a good idea. If you use your lump sum for this, might you then have to borrow to buy something else? This would be foolish: you're getting tax relief on your mortgage which you wouldn't get, for example, on a loan to buy a car. More fundamentally, should you be taking a lump sum at all? You could be losing more in pension that you would be paying out in mortgage payments (see p17 for more on choosing whether or not to take a lump sum).

If you decide to pay off an endowment mortgage early, you also have to decide what to do with the endowment policy. You'll get the best return by making payments for the period originally agreed. But there are two other options; you can:

- *cash in* the policy and get a lump sum or
- make the policy *paid-up*. You stop paying the premiums and the insurance

company reduces the sum of money it guarantees to pay out at the end of the period originally agreed.

=**ACTION**= Ask the insurance company for three figures – the current sum you're guaranteed to get if you continue the policy, the paid-up value and the current cash-in value. You'll probably discover that the sum guaranteed is much higher than either the cash-in or paid-up value.

MOVING HOME

If you decide to live somewhere else, there are many aspects to consider, including:

- the costs involved
- where to go
- what type of property.

Your finances

Get a valuation on your present property, and find out how much property costs in the area you plan to move to. While you might be able to afford to pay cash for your new home, there could be advantages in taking out a mortgage. That way you will release some of the money that's tied up in your present home either to spend or invest for income now or later. You'll also get tax relief on up to £30,000 worth of loans.

What sort of mortgage should you consider? With a new endowment mortgage, the premiums on the life insurance policy would be high because of your age. A repayment mortgage is worth considering, although the lender may be prepared to lend for only 15 years or so, which would make the capital repayments relatively high.

An interest-only mortgage is almost certainly the cheapest way to borrow. You pay the interest, and the loan is repaid from the proceeds of the new home if you move, or from your estate. You are unlikely to be able to borrow more than three quarters of the value of the property (though if you intend to borrow only £30,000, to maximise your tax relief, this shouldn't cause any problems). Get several quotations. If you are a couple, also check that if one of you dies the other will be able to continue with the mortgage and not be forced to move in order to repay the loan.

Before deciding on a particular property, check the likely running costs: heating and maintenance costs, community charge, water charges, service charges (if you are moving to a flat) and insurance.

Also, remember that moving costs themselves are high, including fees for surveyors, solicitors and estate agents, stamp duty, and possibly a Land Registry fee.

Where to go

You may already have an idea of where you want to live in retirement. But be realistic. Remember that the countryside can be bleak in winter, the seaside can be windy and cold, and both can become unpleasant in summer when invaded by hordes of visitors. Ideally, you should spend as much time as possible in the new area, at weekends, during the week, in the summer and in the winter, to try to get some idea of what living there permanently would be like.

Ask yourself:

- How handy are the shops, post office, bank, building society, library, hairdressers?
- How frequent and reliable is the public transport? Are there travel concessions for retired people?
- How close is the nearest doctor, dentist and hospital?

- Do you have friends/relatives in the area?
- Would you easily be able to visit your family and friends – and would they be able to visit you?
- How good are the communications in the area – particularly the roads, railways and buses?
- Would you be happy living there if your partner died?
- What is the weather like in winter?
- If you now regularly go to concerts, cinemas or theatres, will it be as easy in your new location?
- What leisure facilities are available?

For more about the decision-making and problems to do with moving home, consult *Which? Way to Buy, Sell and Move House* (see insert E).

Moving abroad

Living permanently abroad is rather different from being there on holiday. It's even more vital to think through the pros and cons than it is for moving within the UK. Talk to other British people living in the area about the problems and advantages.

Do you speak the language of the country? If not, now's the time to learn – even if you don't become fluent. Bear in mind that you're likely to see less of your family (visits will almost certainly be less frequent), and if you want to visit them, the cost could be high.

Check up on the tax rules. If you have a home in the UK that's available for your use and come back to Britain regularly you are likely to be liable to pay UK taxes even though you live abroad for most of the time. See the latest issue of *Which? Tax-Saving Guide* and the Inland Revenue leaflet IR20 *Residents and Non-residents Liability to Tax in the UK* (from your local Inland Revenue). You can be liable for tax in the country where you are living as well as in your country of origin. But there are various agreements between countries to ensure that any tax you pay on income abroad is set against your UK tax liability.

You can get your state pensions tax-free, anywhere in the world. But the amount you get won't necessarily increase as it would do in the UK. It will increase if you move, for example, to any of the other countries of the European Community, or to Canada, New Zealand, Jamaica or the USA. But if you were to emigrate to Australia, your pension would be frozen. For other countries or further information, consult your local social security office.

You might also want to investigate:

- the facilities for health care that will be available to you and the cost (if any)
- whether you need a permit to live in the country
- whether you'll need a work permit (for instance, if you want to teach English)
- banking arrangements – not only for day-to-day needs, but for transferring money from the UK and so on.

What sort of home?

This is up to you – one person's dream cottage could be another person's hovel. But there are some general points worth considering.

A *detached house* can provide privacy and peace (especially if it has a large garden) but heating bills and maintenance costs are relatively high. A *terraced house* has lower heating bills, but noise can be a problem and the closeness of neighbours can be either a blessing or a nuisance. A *semi-detached house* combines the pros and cons of the other two types.

Many people's ideal is a *bungalow* which has some of the advantages of a detached house, but no stairs (an advantage that increases with your age). The cost of a bungalow is often high when compared with a similar-sized house, mainly because demand tends to exceed supply.

Living in a *flat* has advantages – neighbours close at hand and (in theory) fewer worries about what to do if the roof leaks or the chimney cracks. But while these responsibilities fall on the landlord, or on the managing agent who looks after the building, you have to pay your share towards the cost. And you frequently have little or no say about when or by whom the work will be carried out. Many retired people decide to live in a flat because of the advantages, but don't realise that the financial outlay, particularly on an older block, can be far higher than the occasional expenditure on repairs to their own house, which they can have done when and by whom they choose.

Flats can be in a purpose-built block or in a large house or other building which has been split up and converted. With a flat conversion it's important that your surveyor checks that the conversion work has been properly carried out. In particular, he or she should check how soundproof the walls and ceilings are.

Whatever sort of flat you're buying, make sure you understand the arrangements for (and the cost of) ground rent, service charges, structural repairs and insurance of the building. Have a full survey, not only on your own flat but on the shared structural parts such as the roof. Check with other people in the block what they've had to pay out in recent years. Find out if there is a residents' association – if there is, you stand a better chance of having any complaints investigated. Some blocks or groups of flats are managed by the residents themselves, thereby saving management fees.

Most flats are sold leasehold and you pay ground rent to the freeholder. The main drawback of this is that you are unlikely to get a mortgage if there is less than around 70 years of so of the lease left. But it is now possible for residents to own the freehold of a block, so find out whether this is likely to happen in the flat you're interested in buying.

Council accommodation

If you are renting a council property you may be able to exchange it for something more suitable or in a different area. Locally, you may find it easy to move if you are occupying a home that is larger than you need as the council may even be prepared to give you a grant to persuade you to move somewhere smaller. You can also register with the Tenants' Exchange Scheme, which will make efforts to match your requirements with those of another tenant who wants to move (see insert E in the back pocket). You can also make an independent arrangement with another tenant, though you'd need your council's permission before moving. Also, there's a privately run scheme, Locatex, to help council tenants who want to move to a different area (see sheet E).

Alternatively, retirement might be the time to think seriously about exercising your right to buy your home (particularly if you've been a tenant for many years and expect a lump sum on retirement). Depending on how long you've lived there and the type of property, the discount could be anything up to 60%. Ask your local council for the leaflet *Your Right to Buy a Home*.

SECTION 7

LOOKING TO THE FUTURE

Your needs in later retirement will be different to those of your sixties. While you may not need to take decisions now, it might help your planning to keep your long-term future at the back of your mind. Issues to think about include:

- money
- your home
- making your will and inheritance tax planning.

MONEY

If your occupational pension isn't index-linked, your income in real terms will fall as the years pass. So you may need to plan to boost your income in later years. You could decide to spend your capital, but don't underestimate the amount of money this could use up or the number of years for which you might need the income. If you're 70 and reckon you need an extra £5,000 a year income, in ten years you'll spend around £65,000 even if inflation averages only five per cent.

Buying an annuity

One way of boosting your income would be to invest a lump sum in an annuity. In return for the lump sum, an insurance company pays you an income for life. Part of the income is tax-free as the taxman treats it as your capital which is being returned bit by bit over the years.

The income you get is based on the interest rates at the time you buy the annuity and on your life expectancy: the older you are when you buy an annuity, the higher the income. Men usually get more than women of the same age because they tend to die earlier. In general, you shouldn't be thinking about annuities much before you reach your 70s and a woman might do better to wait until she is in her mid-seventies.

A couple can buy an annuity together, a *joint life and survivor annuity*. This means that the income is paid out until both of you have died – you can arrange either for the income to continue unchanged after the first death, or for it to reduce after it. A joint life and survivor annuity costs more: in effect, it provides a smaller income for the same lump sum.

There are three types of annuity:

- **level**, whereby you get the same income each year
- **increasing**, whereby the income rises each year by a lowish amount, e.g. 5%. This gives some protection against inflation
- **index-linked**, whereby the income increases in line with the rise in prices as measured by the RPI (though the way these annuities are taxed means that your after-tax income won't quite keep pace with inflation).

Although you'll get the highest initial income from a level annuity, inflation will eat away at the buying power of the income, so unless you believe that inflation will be fairly low you would probably do better going for one of other types.

29

The disadvantage of an annuity is that you lose your lump sum; the advantage is that you get a regular income. Weigh these up, bearing in mind what else you might want to do with the lump sum. It would certainly not be wise to spend all your capital on an annuity, but it may be a sensible home for some of it. Finally, if you are in poor health, avoid an annuity and invest your money elsewhere.

Home income plans

Your home is another potential source of income when you get older. Essentially, you get a loan based on the security of your home and use it to buy an annuity. For the rest of your life you get the income from the annuity – after basic rate tax and interest on the loan have been deducted. When you die the loan is repaid from your estate.

You must be at least 70 to be able to take advantage of a home income plan; with a couple, the joint ages usually have to be at least 150. And you have to own your own home – either freehold, or on a long lease (a minimum of between 50 and 80 years, depending on the company).

With some plans, the interest rate and the income from the annuity are fixed when you take out the loan. However, there are also *variable interest* plans whereby the interest you pay on the loan varies in line with interest rates in general. These are best avoided as your income will fluctuate with interest rates.

You should also be wary of schemes which add (or 'roll-up') the interest to the loan so that you don't pay anything and get the annuity in full. While your income will be high, the total owing could eventually be more than the value of your home so that you would be forced to sell up, or pay interest on the whole outstanding sum.

You would get a better after-tax income by paying cash for an annuity than by subscribing to a home income plan. But one is worth considering if you need extra income and have a valuable home and few, if any, other resources. If you want to move you can transfer the plan to your new property. However, if you don't buy another property but move into a nursing home, say, you'll have to repay the loan. But you'll still get the income from the annuity and won't be paying interest on the loan, so you will be better off.

Age Concern can provide information on home income plans (see insert E).

Reversion schemes

With these schemes you sell all or part of your home in return for a lump sum or annuity and the right to remain there until you die. You may have to sell your home for as little as half its actual worth and from then on any increase in its value will belong to the company and none of it to you. In addition you will be responsible for paying for repairs. All in all, it's best to steer clear of such schemes.

YOUR HOME

In the early years of retirement the chances are high that you will be fit and active. And indeed this happy state of affairs could continue for many years. But in time most people find themselves slowing down physically and begin to find what used to be straightforward everyday activities a bit of a struggle. With forethought you could carry out improvements and alterations to your home before, or in the early years of retirement, or take your future requirements into account when choosing a new home. Not only will you save money but you will also be prepared for the time when you need a little more help around the home.

Safety, security and convenience are the things to look for. For example, it can save a lot of bending to have electric sockets in convenient places and at a reasonable height – above the work surface in the kitchen, at waist height in living rooms etc. Make sure that there are plenty of sockets in each room to avoid trailing flex, and that there's enough lighting, especially on stairs.

In the bathroom, think about putting a handrail over the bath (it'll be of use to younger people too). Some baths are more suitable than others for older people – for example some have lower than usual sides, a 'seat' or a lower section in the middle of one side. If you don't have a downstairs lavatory, consider having one installed with a basin and perhaps even a shower.

In the kitchen, shelves and cupboards are often fitted too high or too low, which makes for a lot of stretching or bending. If you're planning a new kitchen, bear this is mind; if you're adapting your current one, have more cupboards fitted at sensible heights so you don't need to use the others. A split-level oven can be mounted at a reasonable height so that you don't have to stoop.

Smoke alarms are inexpensive and can be fitted easily. You should also consider keeping a fire blanket near the cooker and perhaps even a fire extinguisher. Security can be improved in many homes by fitting good window and door locks. Outside lighting to illuminate night-time visitors is worth considering; and a burglar alarm might be a good idea if you have a lot of valuables. Contact the local police station and ask the crime prevention officer to come to your home and advise on how to make it more secure.

Re-planning the garden could ensure you can cope with it for longer. While you might not like the idea of borders full of shrubs, heathers and conifers, at least these need less maintenance than bedding plants.

Sheltered housing

As you get older you might feel you want to move somewhere that has been designed for people in their later years. Sheltered housing (also known as retirement homes) is for the healthy elderly. It allows you to carry on living independently but provides help in case of emergencies. You no longer have the worries associated with running and maintaining your own home. However, although you will not be directly involved in decisions about cleaning or decorating, for example, you will have to contribute to the cost.

You can buy sheltered accommodation on a leasehold basis (or you may be able to rent it from a private developer, housing association or local authority). In general you have to be at least 55 or 60 (depending on the terms of the lease) and you must be in good health. As the market for sheltered housing is quite new, and more people are living longer, there is great demand for places and you may have to be put on a waiting list.

Before committing yourself find out:

- What is the minimum age? If you buy when you are younger can you sub-let until you reach the minimum age?
- Can you have friends or relatives to stay in your unit or is there a guest room? For how long can a guest stay and how much will it cost?

- During what hours is the warden on duty and what cover is there for when he or she is off duty?
- What happens if you become ill?
- When (or if) you decide to sell, can you choose your purchaser, or does the landlord do so?; if the latter, what commission will be charged?
- Can you choose how much to sell for, and what deductions will be made by the landlord in the event of your selling?
- How much is the ground rent and how often does it increase?
- How much are the service charges and what do they cover? How will they increase? Is this laid down in the lease or is there no control?
- How are repairs and improvements paid for and do you have any choice in the sort of work that will be carried out?

Age Concern publishes a booklet on sheltered housing – see insert E for details.

MAKING A WILL

This is an essential step for everyone. It may seem strange to think about making a will when trying to plan your finances for the future, but a will can do more than ensure that your money and everything else you own goes where you want them to. With planning you can reduce the amount of inheritance tax that will be paid by your heirs when you die.

If the value of what you're leaving is likely to be more than a certain amount there could be inheritance tax to pay (see update sheet F). This total also includes gifts made in the seven years before death. But some gifts made within this time and some bequests are tax-free:

- all gifts and bequests to your spouse
- all gifts and bequests to charities and political parties
- gifts and bequests to certain national institutions (e.g. National Trust, British Museum)
- some gifts of property considered to be part of the national heritage (e.g. buildings, books, paintings) to a non-profit-making body
- small gifts of up to £250 per recipient per year
- wedding presents (up to £5,000 to your children, £2,500 to your grandchildren, £1,000 to anyone else)
- gifts which you make out of your normal income provided they are part of your normal spending and don't reduce your standard of living
- gifts of £3,000 a year which aren't exempt for any other reason.

Detailed advice on making your will and on ways in which you can minimise inheritance tax is included in the companion *Which?* Action Pack *Make Your Will*, available from the address on insert E in the back pocket.